People Pow

Life's Little Lessons on Relationships

by
John C. Maxwell

Honor Books, Inc.
P. O. Box 55388
Tulsa, Oklahoma 74155

Unless otherwise indicated, all scripture quotations are from the *King James Version* of the Bible.

Scripture reference marked NIV is taken from the *Holy Bible, New International Version* ®. NIV ®. Copyright © 1973, 1978, 1984 by International Bible Society. Used by permission of Zondervan Publishing House. All Rights Reserved.

People Power: Life's Little Lessons on Relationship
ISBN 1-56292-035-9
Copyright © 1996 by John C. Maxwell
1530 Jamacha Road, Suite D
El Cajon, California 92019

Published by **Honor Books**
P. O. Box 55388
Tulsa, Oklahoma 74155

Introduction

Millionaire industrialist John D. Rockefeller once said that he was willing to pay more for this quality than for any other ability under the sun. President Theodore Roosevelt said it was the most important ingredient in the formula of success. That quality is our ability to deal with people—relationships. More than almost anything else in life, relationships make or break us.

That's why it's important to keep learning about them. This book is designed as a short course in relationships. May these timeless quotes and insights from men and women who understand people help you do the same.

John C. Maxwell

The Ten Commandments
of Human Relations:

1. Speak to people.
2. Smile at people.
3. Call people by name.
4. Be friendly and helpful.
5. Be cordial.
6. Have a genuine interest in people.
7. Be generous with praise.
8. Be considerate of the feelings of others.
9. Be thoughtful of the opinions of others.
10. Be alert to give service.

Author Unknown

If you're going to play together as a team,
you've got to care for one another.
You've got to love each other.

Vince Lombardi

The Law of Relationship says that every person is merely four people away from any other human on earth.

I don't know the key to success, but the key to failure is trying to please everybody.

Bill Cosby

No matter how much work you
can do, no matter how engaging
your personality may be,
you will not advance far in business
if you cannot work through others.

John Craig

You can't be any closer to God
than you are to the person you love least.

———

You can't make the other fellow feel
important in your presence if you
secretly feel that he is a nobody.

Les Giblin

It is very easy to forgive others
their mistakes; it takes more grit
and gumption to forgive them
for having witnessed your own.

Jessamyn West

People aren't sales resistant—
they are salespeople resistant.

Mark Hebenstreit

Numbers don't mean anything...
because it's people that count.

Will Rogers

$$R + R - R = R + R$$
(Rules and Regulations
minus Relationships equals
Resentment and Rebellion)

A drop of honey catches more flies
than a gallon of gall.

Abraham Lincoln

Friendship flourishes at
the fountain of forgiveness.

William A. Ward

If someone hurts you,
first try to figure out whether
that hurt was intentional or not.
Not every hurt is an attack.

Getting people to like you
is merely the other side of liking them.

———

Ninety percent of the friction of daily life
is caused by the wrong tone of voice.

It is well to remember
that the entire population of the
universe with one trifling exception
is composed of others.

J. A. Holmes

PEOPLE POWER

If you want to get along with people,
pretend you never knew
whatever they tell you.

———

Each relationship nurtures
a strength or a weakness within you.

16

Few things will pay you bigger dividends
than the time and trouble
you take to understand people.
Almost nothing will add more to your
stature as an executive and a person.
Nothing will give you greater satisfaction
or bring you more happiness.

Kienzle & Dare

Do to others
as you would have them do to you.

Jesus (Luke 6:31)

A great man shows his greatness
for the way he treats little men.

Thomas Carlyle

If you want to lose friends quickly,
start bragging about yourself;
if you want to make and keep friends,
start bragging about others.

I will speak ill of no man
and speak all the good I know
of everybody.

Benjamin Franklin

The true test of being comfortable with
someone else is the ability to share silence.

Frank Tyger

The man who goes alone can start the day.
But he who travels with another
must wait until the other is ready.

Henry David Thoreau

Relationships are not formed but forged.

Anyone who loves his opinions
more than he does his brethren
will defend his opinions and
destroy his brethren.

Let another man praise thee,
and not thine own mouth;
a stranger, and not thine own lips.

Proverbs 27:2

You cannot shake hands
with a clenched fist.

Indira Gandhi

To handle yourself, use your head.
To handle others, use your heart.

John Maxwell

Ninety percent of the art of living consists of getting along with people you cannot stand.

Samuel Goldwyn

Instead of putting others in their place,
put yourself in their place.

Every man is entitled to be valued
by his best moments.

Ralph Waldo Emerson

PEOPLE POWER

Natural talent, intelligence, a wonderful education — none of these guarantees success. Something else is needed: The sensitivity to understand what other people want and the willingness to give it to them.

John Luther

27

One man working with you
is worth a dozen men working for you.

Herman M. Koelliker

People don't care how much you know
until they know how much you care.

John Maxwell

If you would win a man to your cause,
first convince him that you
are his sincere friend.

Abraham Lincoln

The most important single ingredient
in the formula of success is knowing
how to get along with people.

Theodore Roosevelt

I will pay more for the ability
to deal with people than for any
other ability under the sun.

John D. Rockefeller

There is a rule in sailing
that the more maneuverable ship
should give way to the less
maneuverable craft.
I think this is sometimes a good rule
to follow in human relationships as well.

Dr. Joyce Brothers

If you are suffering from a bad man's
injustice, forgive him
lest there be two bad men.

Augustine

Seek to be a plow rather than a bulldozer.
The plow cultivates the soil,
making it a good place for seed to grow.
The bulldozer scrapes the earth
and pushes every obstacle out of the way.

A Short Course in Human Relations...

The Six Most Important Words:
"I admit I made a mistake."
The Five Most Important Words: "You did a good job."
The Four Most Important Words:
"What is your opinion?"
The Three Most Important Words: "If you please."
The Two Most Important Words: "Thank You."
The Most Important Word: "We."
The Least Important Word: "I."

Author Unknown

Don't use your people to build
a great work; use your work
to build a great people.
Jack Hyles

There is no more noble occupation in the
world than to assist another human being
— to help someone succeed.
Alan Loy McGinnis

Practice the 101 percent principle:
Find the 1 thing you agree on with
another person, and then give it 100
percent of your encouragement.

John Maxwell

Assets make things possible.
People make things happen.

———

You can tell more about a person
by what he says about others than
you can by what others say about him.

It is one of the most beautiful
compensations of this life
that no man can sincerely try to help
another without helping himself.

Ralph Waldo Emerson

In getting along with others,
98 percent depends on
our behavior with others.

———

Marriage is the only union that
can't be organized.
Both sides think they're management.

Funny Funny World

If you would have a happy life,
remember two things: In matters
of principle, stand like a rock;
in matters of taste,
swim with the current.

Thomas Jefferson

We never know the love of our parents
for us till we have become parents.

Henry Ward Beecher

My most brilliant achievement
was my ability to be able to persuade
my wife to marry me.

Winston Churchill

Two are better than one,
because they have a good return
for their work:
If one falls down, his friend
can help him up.
But pity the man who falls and
has no one to help him up!

Ecclesiastes 4:9-10 NIV

Even marriages made in heaven
need down-to-earth maintenance work.

Lloyd Byers

It is not marriage that fails,
it is people that fail. All that marriage
does is to show people up.

Harry Emerson Fosdick

To keep the fire burning brightly,
keep the two logs together,
near enough to keep each other warm,
and far enough apart—about a finger's
breadth—for breathing room.
Good fire, good marriage—same rule.

Marnie Reed Crowell

God is the only third party in a marriage
that can make it work.

———

Faith makes all things possible.
Love makes all things easy.
Hope makes all things work.

Before a marriage,
a man will lie awake all night
thinking about something you said;
after marriage, he'll fall asleep
before you finish saying it.

Helen Rowland

The key to a perfect marriage
is not expecting perfection.

Marriage is an empty box.
It remains empty unless you
put in more than you take out.

Love at first sight is nothing special.
It's when two people have been
looking at each other for years
that it becomes a miracle.

Sam Levinson

Courtship brings out the best.
Marriage brings out the rest.

Cullen Hightower

Love will find a way.
Indifference will find an excuse.

There are two great motivators in life.
One is fear. The other is love.
You can lead an organization by fear,
but if you do, you will ensure
that people won't perform up to
their real capabilities.

Jan Carlson

We may not choose whom we will love
if we claim to be Christians.

———

A person needs to be loved the most
when he deserves to be loved the least.

The biggest disease today is not
leprosy or tuberculosis,
but rather the feeling of being unwanted,
uncared for, and deserted by everybody.

Mother Teresa

Truth without love is brutality.
Love without truth is hypocrisy.

———

The love of our neighbor is the only door
out of the dungeon of self.

George MacDonald

Genuine love is a fragile flower.
It must be maintained and protected
if it is to survive.
Love can perish...when there is
no time for romantic activity...
when a man and his wife forget
how to talk to each other.

James Dobson

Faults are thick where love is thin.

———

The law of love always supersedes
the law of personal liberty.

You will find as you look back upon your life that the moments when you have really lived are the moments when you have done things in the spirit of love.

Henry Drummond

If you want to make your mother happy,
talk to her. If you want to make
your father happy, listen.

———

Human beings are the only creatures
on earth that allow their children
to come back home.

Bill Cosby

How far you go in life depends on
your being tender with the young,
compassionate with the aged,
sympathetic with the striving,
and tolerant of the weak and the strong.
Because some day in life you will
have been all of these.

George Washington Carver

A man should choose for his wife
the woman he would choose as his best
friend, were she a man.

There is no lonelier person than the one
who lives with a spouse with whom
he or she cannot communicate.

Margaret Mead

When I'm getting ready to reason with a
man, I spend one-third of my time
thinking about myself
and what I am going to say —
and two-thirds thinking about him
and what he is going to say.

Abraham Lincoln

People are lonely because
they build walls instead of bridges.

Joseph F. Newton

———◆———

It's when you rub elbows
with a man that you find out
what he has up his sleeve.

To keep your marriage brimming,
With love in the loving cup,
When you're wrong, admit it.
When you're right, shut up.

Ogden Nash

Successful marriage is always a triangle:
a man, a woman, and God.

Cecil Myers

Train up a child in the way he should go—
and walk there yourself once in a while.

Josh Billings

Parents are prone to give their children
everything except the one
thing they need most.
That is time.

Emma K. Hulburt

Never try to make your son or daughter another you; one is enough!

Arnold Glasow

The best gift a father can give to his son is the gift of himself—his time.

C. Neil Strait

The most important thing that parents
can teach their children
is how to get along without them.

Frank A. Clark

By the time we realize our parents
may have been right,
we usually have children
who think we are wrong.

There is no more lovely, friendly
and charming relationship,
communion or company
than a good marriage.

Martin Luther

God chooses our relatives;
we choose our friends.

———

Never be yoked to one
who refuses the yoke of Christ.

The formula for achieving a successful
relationship is simple:
You should treat all disasters
as if they were trivialities,
but never treat a triviality as if
it were a disaster.

Quentin Crisp

Most communication problems
can be solved with proximity.

———

Man and melons are hard to know.

Benjamin Franklin

A gossip is one who talks
to you about others;
a bore is one who talks
to you about himself;
and a brilliant conversationalist
is one who talks to you about yourself.

Lisa Kirk

A person whose ship has come in
usually finds most of his
relatives at the dock.

—◆—

The harder you work at a relationship,
the harder it is to surrender.

The opinions which we hold
of one another, our relationships
with friends and kinsfolk
are in no sense permanent,
save in appearance, but are
as eternally fluid as the sea itself.

Marcel Proust

A man is known by
the company he organizes.

Ambrose Pierce

A wise man associating with the vicious
becomes an idiot; a dog traveling with
good men becomes a rational being.

Arabic Proverb

You will acquire the vices and virtues
of your closest associates.
The fragrance of their lives
will pervade your life.

John Maxwell

Tell me thy company,
and I'll tell thee what thou art.

Cervantes

Every man is like the company
he is wont to keep.

Euripides

In choosing a friend, go up a step.

Jewish Proverb

A wise man may look ridiculous
in the company of fools.

Thomas Fuller

He that lies down with dogs
shall rise up with flies.

Latin Proverb

It is better to weep with wise men
than to laugh with fools.

Spanish Proverb

Familiarity breeds contempt —
and children.

Mark Twain

———

Satan's friendship reaches
to the prison door.

Turkish Proverb

We cannot forgive another
for not being ourselves.

Ralph Waldo Emerson

None knows the weight
of another's burden.

Thomas Fuller

Just as much as we see in others
we have in ourselves.

William Hazlitt

Most often it happens that one attributes
to others only the feelings of which
one is capable oneself.

André Gide

The longer we live,
the more we find
we are like other persons.

Oliver Wendell Holmes

Hurting people hurt people.

John Maxwell

No man is much pleased with a
companion who does not increase,
in some respect, his fondness of himself.

Samuel Johnson

Love or perish.

One learns peoples through the heart,
not the eyes or the intellect.

Mark Twain

Don't drown the man who
taught you to swim.
If you learned your trade
or profession from the man,
do not set up in opposition to him.

C. H. Spurgeon

It is a wise father that
knows his own child.

Shakespeare

What the mother sings to the cradle
goes all the way down to the coffin.

Henry Ward Beecher

It is the atmosphere created
primarily by the mother
that makes a home worthwhile.

J. R. Bookhoff

A father is a banker provided by nature.

French Proverb

You don't have to deserve
your mother's love.
You have to deserve your father's.
He's more particular.

Robert Frost

Where parents do too much
for their children,
the children will not do much
for themselves.

Elbert Hubbard

An angry father is most
cruel toward himself.

Publius Syrus

———◆———

Every beetle is a gazelle
in the eyes of its mother.

Moorish Proverb

Romance fails us and so do friendships,
but the relationship of parent and child,
less noisy than all others,
remains indelible and indestructible,
the strongest relationship on earth.

Theodore Reik

There is scarcity of friendship,
but not of friends.

Thomas Fuller

Acquaintance, n. A person whom we know
well enough to borrow from,
but not well enough to lend to.

Ambrose Pierce

A companion loves some agreeable qualities which a man may possess, but a friend loves the man himself.

James Boswell

It is by forgiving that one is forgiven.

Mother Teresa

A man should keep his friendship
in constant repair.

Samuel Johnson

Forsake not an old friend,
for a new one does not
compare with him.

Apocrypha

Between friends there is
no need of justice.

Artistotle

Of all the things granted by wisdom,
none is greater or better than friendship.

Pietro Aretino

Friendship is a strong habitual inclination in two persons to promote the good and happiness of one another.

Eustace Budgell

Wishing to be friends is quick work,
but friendship is a slow-ripening fruit.

Aristotle

Faithful are the wounds of a friend;
but the kisses of an enemy are deceitful.

Proverbs 27:6

The firmest friendships have been
formed in mutual adversity,
as iron is most strongly united
by the fiercest flame.

Charles Caleb Colton

True friendship is like sound health;
the value of it is seldom known
until it be lost.

Charles Caleb Colton

Friendship makes prosperity
more brilliant, and lightens adversity
by dividing and sharing it.

Cicero

The friendships which last are those wherein each friend respects the other's dignity to the point of not really wanting anything from him.

Cyril Connolly

The real friendships among men
are so rare that when they occur
they are famous.

Clarence Day

It is one of the blessings of old friends
that you can afford to be
stupid with them.

Ralph Waldo Emerson

Real friendship is shown
in times of trouble;
prosperity is full of friends.

Euripides

The only way to have a friend
is to be one.

Ralph Waldo Emerson

⚊✦⚊

One loyal friend is worth
ten thousand relatives.

Euripides

A friend is a person
with whom I may be sincere.
Before him, I may think aloud.

Ralph Waldo Emerson

A good friend
is my nearest relation.

Thomas Fuller

Friendship multiplies the good of life
and divides the evil.

Baltasar Gracian

A friend may well be reckoned
the masterpiece of nature.

Ralph Waldo Emerson

A sympathetic friend
can be quite as dear as a brother.

Homer

Your friend is a man who knows
all about you, and still likes you.

Elbert Hubbard

Love is rarer than genius itself.
And friendship is rarer still.

Charles Peguy

A true friend
is the greatest of all blessings.

La Rochefoucauld

Hold a true friend with both your hands.

Nigerian Proverb

The proper office of a friend
is to side with you
when you are in the wrong.
Nearly anybody will side with you
when you are in the right.

Mark Twain

Friendship either finds or makes equals.

Publius Syrus

—■◆■—

A man cannot be said to succeed in this life who does not satisfy one friend.

Henry David Thoreau

You cannot be friends upon any other terms than upon the terms of equality.

Woodrow Wilson

Whoso findeth a wife
findeth a good thing.

Proverbs 18:22

—◦—◂▣▸—◦—

Can two walk together,
except they be agreed?

Amos 3:3

Marriage is the perfection
which love aimed at,
ignorant of what it sought.

Ralph Waldo Emerson

A rare spoil for a man is the
winning of a good wife.

Euripides

Only a person who has faith in himself
is able to be faithful to others.

Erich Fromm

There is nothing nobler or more admirable than when two people who see eye to eye keep house as man and wife, confounding their enemies and delighting their friends.

Homer

A man's best fortune,
or his worst, is his wife.

Thomas Fuller

The love we have in our youth is
superficial compared to the love
that an old man has for his old wife.

Will Durant (On his 90th birthday)

A man should be taller,
older, heavier, uglier,
and hoarser than his wife.

Edgar Watson Howe

Man's best asset is a sympathetic wife.

Euripides

An ideal wife is any woman
who has an ideal husband.

Booth Tarkington

There are six requisites
in every happy marriage.
The first is Faith
and the remaining five
are Confidence.

Elbert Hubbard

Every mother is like Moses.
She does not enter the promised land.
She prepares a world she will not see.

Pope Paul VI

Back of every achievement is a proud wife
and a surprised mother-in-law.

Brooks Hays

No man knows what the wife of his bosom is until he has gone with her through the fiery trials of this world.

Washington Irving

There is more pleasure in loving
than in being beloved.

Thomas Fuller

We should measure affection,
not like youngsters by the ardor of our
passion, but by its strength and constancy.

Cicero

A successful marriage
requires falling in love many times,
always with the same person.

Mignon McLaughlin

Give every man thine ear,
but few thy voice.

Shakespeare

Most Americans don't,
in any vital sense, get together;
they only do things together.

Louis Kronberger

Never speak of yourself to others;
make them talk about themselves instead:
therein lies the whole art of pleasing.
Everyone knows it and everyone forgets it.

Edmond and Jules de Goncourt

A single arrow is easily broken,
but not ten in a bundle.

Japanese Proverb

Behold, how good and how pleasant it is
for brethren to dwell together in unity!

Psalm 133:1

The holy passion of friendship
is so sweet and steady
and loyal and enduring in nature
that it will last through a whole lifetime,
if not asked to lend money.

Mark Twain

Whoso loves believes the impossible.

Elizabeth Barrett Browning

———❖———

Many waters cannot quench love,
neither can the floods drown it.

Song of Solomon 8:7

Love means giving one's self to another
person fully, not just physically.
When two people really love each other,
this helps them to stay alive and grow.
One must really be loved to grow.

Nancy Reagan

Love is the true price of love.

George Herbert

The course of love
never did run smooth.

Shakespeare

Greater love
hath no man than this,
that a man lay down his life
for his friends.

Jesus (John 15:13)

If you've never been hated by your child,
you've never been a parent.

Bette Davis

⚊⚋⚊

I have found the best way to give
advice to your children
is to find out what they want
and then advise them to do it.

Harry S. Truman

I talk and talk and talk,
and I haven't taught people
in 50 years what my father taught
by example in one week.

Mario Cuomo

The most important thing a father can do
for his children is to love their mother.

Theodore M. Hesburgh

Every generation revolts against its fathers
and makes friends with its grandfathers.

Lewis Mumford

Build me a son, O Lord,
who will be strong enough to know
when he is weak, and brave enough
to face himself when he is afraid,
one who will be proud and unbending
in honest defeat, and humble
and gentle in victory.

Prayer of Douglas MacArthur

Other things may change us,
but we start and end with family.

Anthony Brandt

You don't choose your family.
They are God's gift to you,
as you are to them.

Desmond Tutu

In the next year or so,
my signature will appear on
$60 billion of United States currency.
More important to me, however,
is the signature that appears on my life—
the strong, proud, assertive handwriting
of a loving father and mother.

Katherine D. Ortega, U.S. Treasurer

We need a better family life
to make us better servants of the people.

Jimmy Carter

Spoil your husband, but don't spoil your
children—that's my philosophy.

Louise Sevier Giddings Currey
(1961 New York Post Mother of the Year)

President Johnson and I
have a lot in common.
We were both born in small towns...
and we're both fortunate in the fact
that we think we married above ourselves.

Richard M. Nixon

Success in marriage does not come
merely through finding the right mate,
but through being the right mate.

Barnett Brickner

Marriage is not just spiritual communion
and passionate embraces;
marriage is also three-meals-a-day
and remembering to carry out the trash.

Dr. Joyce Brothers

The family
is one of nature's
masterpieces.

George Santayana

Bringing up a family
should be an adventure.

Milton R. Sapirstein

Our children are not going to be just
"our children" — they are going to be
other people's husbands and wives
and the parents of our grandchildren.

Mary S. Calderone

A boy becomes an adult three years
before his parents think he does,
and about two years after
he thinks he does.

Lewis B. Hershey

Parenthood remains the greatest single preserve of the amateur.

Alvin Toffler

More than in any other human relationship, overwhelmingly more, motherhood means being instantly interruptible, responsive, responsible.

Tillie Olsen

Friendship with oneself is all-important,
because without it one cannot be friends
with anyone else in the world.

Eleanor Roosevelt

Once you get people laughing,
they're listening and you can tell them
almost anything.

Herbert Gardner

A person reveals his character by nothing
so clearly as the joke he resents.

G. C. Lichtenberg

Among those whom I like,
I can find no common denominator,
but among those whom I love,
I can; all of them make me laugh.

W. H. Auden

As iron sharpens iron, so one man
sharpens another.

Proverbs 27:17 NIV

If a man does not
make new acquaintances
as he advances through life,
he will soon find himself left alone.

Samuel Johnson

When the character of a man is
not clear to you, look at his friends.

Japanese Proverb

Be wiser than other people,
if you can, but do not tell them so.

Lord Chesterfield

Sometimes it's worse to win
a fight than to lose.

Billie Holiday

A friend can tell you
things you don't want to tell yourself.

Frances Ward Weller

The richer your friends,
the more they will cost you.

Elisabeth Marbury

If you want to grow up, go up.
Associate with people whose achievements
exceed your own and model
the growth you desire.

John Maxwell

No man is an island entire of itself;
every man is a part of the continent,
a part of the main.

John Donne

Love all, trust a few.
Do wrong to none.

Shakespeare

If there is anything better
than being loved, it's loving.

Though one may be overpowered,
two can defend themselves.
A cord of three strands
is not quickly broken.

Ecclesiastes 4:12 NIV

Additional copies of this book and other Honor Books
are available from your local bookstore.

Leadership 101, by John C. Maxwell

You Can't Be a Smart Cookie if You Have a Crummy Attitude,
by John C. Maxwell

P. O. Box 55388
Tulsa, OK 74155